KINGDOM MADNESS

WHERE MIRACLES HAPPEN

ANTHONY TUCKER SR.

ANTHONY TUCKER SR.

Copyright © 2020 by Anthony Tucker.

All rights reserved.

No part of this book may be reproduced or transmitted in any form or by any means, electronic or mechanical, including photocopying, recording, or by any information storage and retrieval system, without permission in writing from the copyright author, except for the use of brief quotations in a book review.

Published in the United States by
Pen2Pad Ink Publishing.
www.pen2padink.org

ISBN: 978-1-970135-54-1 Paperback
        978-1-970135-53-4 Hardcover
        978-1-970135-55-8 Ebook

Requests to publish work from this book or to contact the author should be sent to:
atucker@ipodministry.org

Anthony Tucker retains the
rights to all images

Interior design: Pen2Pad Ink Publishing

ANTHONY TUCKER SR.

CONTENTS

Introduction.. 7
Chapter 1: *Off Season*............................... 9
Chapter 2: *The Kingdom Playbook*....... 14
Chapter 3: *Defense*................................. 19
Chapter 4: *Assist*..................................... 22
Chapter 5: *Tempo*................................... 25
Chapter 6: *Execution*.............................. 29
Chapter 7: *All In*..................................... 33
Chapter 8: *The Mindset of The Underdog*................................. 38
Chapter 9: *Winners Make Adjustments*...42
Chapter 10: *Fatigued But Focused*......... 47
Chapter 11: *Expect The Unexpected*..... 52
Chapter 12: *Turnovers*............................ 57
Chapter 13: *Beware of The Cheers*........ 62
Chapter 14: *One Shot*............................. 65
Chapter 15: *Crowning Moment*............. 68
Special Thanks.. 71
Get Connected.. 73
Reference... 74

ANTHONY TUCKER SR.

INTRODUCTION

I will admit that my love for God is undeniable, but my love for basketball is a close second. There is something about this sport that helps me know that hard work has its rewards. It's almost parallel to the same ideals and values that come with worshipping God.

I find it funny that there are thousands of people who attend sports events. They enjoy watching those who practice, plan, and execute on a gridiron, a court, a field, or a block of ice. I can't help but to wonder, how can we can get people to understand that a relationship with God can be just as enjoyable as the Los Angeles Lakers playing the Golden State Warriors?

This book takes one of the most exciting times in basketball and meshes it with how to develop a spiritual relationship with God. I cannot say that this book is the ultimate answer to the aforementioned question, but it is definitely a start that can help those who enjoy the world of hoops and those who are trying to develop a significant relationship with Christ. I pray that this book helps you see how great HE really is.

Pastor Anthony Tucker

CHAPTER 1

OFF SEASON

"The great players show how much they want to play during the offseason — when it's hot, when it's tough, and when no one is watching."

~Tony Alfonso

For four weeks in the month of March in the United States, unknown unrecognizable young men from all across America have an opportunity to become household names in the realm of college basketball. This season is called "March Madness". College basketball teams who have won the most amount of games or their conference tournaments are put into a HUGE bracket to compete against other teams in other conferences. Some schools will be highly recognizable due to their consistent presence in "March Madness". Some schools will force you to google who they are and where they are from.

The madness starts and there they are...unknown and unranked underdogs. Young men from various schools fly under the radar all year long. This tournament puts them on center stage. It's literally pure madness.

To truly understand and define "madness", it must be put in a proper perspective. In a way, the intensity and excitement that occurs during "March Madness" is often compared to the "madness" that occurs in the Kingdom of God.

Yes, the kingdom of God is definitely a crazy place. I say this because, in the kingdom, there are so many people that we teach and preach about in the Bible that are uplifting and motivating people. They are people that man did not consider worthy to even be used by God. Moses had a speech impediment, yet God wanted his voice to speak instructions to his people. Rahab was known as the harlot. Surely, no one was going to consider her for kingdom work, but we see in the big picture she played a major role assisting the kingdom movement.

You may say, "I don't do religion,

politics, sports, or entertainment." That is understandable. However, in everyday life, you must have the same mindset. Let's say for example that you do not have a degree. As a matter of fact, no one in your family has a degree. You may get upset or depressed because you see others with degrees "moving on up" like the Jefferson's, and you are still in the same place. This is not necessarily a bad thing.

The good news is that God's path for you is not the same as everyone else's. An opportunity may arise for you to make the same or more as those with the degrees even though you do not have it. The insane 'madness' in life is, credentials are outwardly seen, but your capabilities with God are inwardly known. He will make all things are possible.

"Kingdom Madness" is a true example of Personality over Profile. March Madness is so exciting because the basketball committee selects teams based not on the team's profile and NOT fan approval like some other sports. The team's personality is what carried them through the rollercoaster ride all season. The teams persevere enough to get into "March Madness" where miracles happen.

Miss Universe 2019 winner, Zozibini

Tunzi, made an alarming statement after her victory. She said prior to the competition, people strongly suggested and tried to persuade her to wear a wig so she could fit the profile better. Ms. Tunzi, who proudly represents South Africa, said no. She wanted to wear her natural hair and show that beauty does not come in a certain profile. She wanted to inspire little girls and women worldwide to be their authentic selves.

In the off season basketball players continue to eat healthy, work out consistently, and study their craft to build their mental and physical strength. In your spiritual life you can use these same practices. You have to fast, pray, study the word of God, and meditate on the scriptures to build a solid foundation and relationship with God.

Be empowered. Be enlightened. Be encouraged. Utilize the God-given ability and personality that HE has placed in you to be victorious. Man wants to change you to fit his profile. God wants you as you are for HIS purpose.

Kingdom Nugget: Just because you appear to be an underdog right now or you're currently in your off season doesn't mean a champion doesn't dwell within you. You don't have to be seen or known to be used by God. He does not call the qualified. He qualifies those that HE calls.

"But God has chosen the foolish things of the world to put to shame the wise, and God has chosen the weak things of the world to put to shame the things which are mighty; and the [a]base things of the world and the things which are despised God has chosen, and the things which are not, to bring to nothing the things that are, that no flesh should glory in His presence."

1 Corinthians 1:27-29

CHAPTER 2

THE KINGDOM PLAYBOOK

"A winner is someone who recognizes his God-given talents, works his tail off to develop them into skills, and uses these skills to accomplish his goals."

~Larry Bird

The teams who make it to "March Madness" did not make it there by mistake or luck. It took practice, drive, and resilience to get them to where they are today. However, it all started with a plan from their coach.

Coaches play the role of a leader. They create the plan to help their players mentally and physically prepare for their opponents. As they are preparing their players, they develop different ideas of how their players can act on the court in order to play to win.

These ideas are usually a part of a coach's playbook.

In "Kingdom Madness", God is our coach and the Bible is our playbook. It is composed of numerous stories and instructions that help us all understand how to handle problems and situations in our lives.

Kingdom Madness has several key principles. Here are some directly from HIS playbook that you should consider:

Giving sacrifice: Every great March madness team that wins in March made personal sacrifices to reach a victory that cannot be seen at the time. During the process the seed is not visible. That sacrifice is a seed that you give. It is working underground. You must plant it, then put the work and time in that is required in order for your seed to grow. The process is preparing you for the big picture. The setbacks that occur during the process are creating an opportunity for you to practice better. Those losses are intended to create an intense hunger for victory.

You have to reach deep down within yourself and push beyond the pain, pressure, and problems in the game of life. When you choose to give of yourself, your sacrifices help to cultivate the end goal: your vision, your dream, and your Kingdom living. Eventually you will see and experience the harvest of a seed. The harvest will be evident in crunch time.

Giving Attention to details: When paying attention to details it's pinpointing and figuring out what's working for you and what's not. As a coach they possess the ability to see things that we can't as players and adjust the team accordingly.

Just as its God's responsibility to pay attention to pay attention to everything that's happening and guide us in the right direction. Is our responsibility to make sure that no matter what's happening in our lives we can recognize our coaches voice, hear the plays being called, and follow the instructions being given.

In making these small adjustments it transitions us into becoming champions and conquerors. Some of us forget to pay attention to the little things about us because our gifts of natural talent and ability to overpower our train of thought. We think to ourselves, "I do not need to practice this because I can do these other things so well." The danger in doing this is what you fail to work on will eventually be exactly what we need to succeed.

Therefore, start paying attention and evaluating you life early. Look to see what's hindering us? what's stopping us? Are there people we are giving to much attention to? Are there people in our life who don't mean us well that we need to get rid of?

The following are additional details in life that we often overlook:

1. We fail to pray.
2. We fail to acknowledge God.
3. We fail to be grateful.

Choosing to fail at these aspects of our life walk with HIM, can lead to making choices that are productive to our success. So, take the time to work on all of you and not just your strengths.

Giving Thanks: Proverbs 3:6 says, "In all thy ways acknowledge him and HE will direct thy path." Thankfulness in this "madness" goes such a long way in helping you develop who you are and your relationship with HIM. It is hard sometimes because of earthly setbacks that you may or may not be able to control. However, during everything attempting to go awry, give thanks. Before you give attention to drama, flaws, and negativity, give thanks. Give thanks that you are where you are with an opportunity to go forward. Be thankful for whatever it is you have and what is to come.

Remember this: Whoever sows sparingly will also reap sparingly, and whoever sows generously will also reap generously. Each of you should give what you have decided in your heart to give, not reluctantly or under compulsion, for God loves a cheerful giver. And God is able to bless you abundantly, so that in all things at all times, having all that you need, you will abound in every good work.

2 Corinthians 9: 6-8

Kingdom Nugget: Give what you can and God's playbook can help with the rest.

CHAPTER 3

DEFENSE

"Great players... are defensive stoppers – they stop their man as well as help teammates. They do the things offensive players HATE!"

~Alan Stein

Defense! Defense! It is a familiar chant you'll hear in most competitive events. The most faithful and loyal fans understand that, no matter how exciting it was to witness all the offense, you must have defense.

Defense means to defend that which you value. How do you defend? First, you must study the opposing team because they have certain tendencies that are particular trends paused for an advantage over you. Second, you must have a passion for what you are defending. Third, you must have a "nose for the ball". In other words, you must have an instinct to take or cause turn overs. Turnovers lead to points that can add more momentum to what you already obtained. It takes being alert when others are walking through the motions, you are turning up the heat. That's defense.

I noticed in "March Madness" how every statistic is glorifies and highlights offensive plays and players. What about defense? One good observation is that the defensive play that has good results in March Madness is focused on being fruitful and not fancy. They desire to be productive and not popular.

When I think about it, Jesus was probably one of the greatest defensive players to ever walk this Earth. His intention was never to be popular or fancy. He simply wanted to do His father's work the best way He could. Take for example Jesus' encounter with Satan on the mountain. (Matt. 4: 1-11; Mark 1: 1-13; Luke 1: 1-14) Jesus knew that Satan was going to do everything He could to break his concentration. So, Jesus fasted for 40 days to build His strength. Jesus' passion for others allowed Him to use His father help and tap into that power when Satan attempted to make him sin.

KINGDOM MADNESS

You fight and work hard for what you accomplish in life whether it is your education, your marriage, or your health. The same tenacity must be applied to protect and preserve. "March Madness" may be a game, but kingdom madness is your life. You must defend what you have been blessed with. You must defend truth verses lies. You must defend right verses wrong. You must defend good versus evil. You must put more effort in defending that which is ours.

Kingdom Nugget: The key to good offense is good defense.

"Therefore take up the whole armor of God, that you may be able to withstand in the evil day, and having done all, to stand firm."

Ephesians 6: 13 (ESV)

CHAPTER 4

ASSIST

"I'll take an assist any day over points."

~Deron Williams

To assist means to help, serve, support, or to give a helping hand to someone. In the NBA Bobby Hurley who is not an incredibly famous NBA player is the current record holder for most assist in the National Collegiate Athletic Association (NCAA) with 1,076 assists during his college career. Most of those assists helped his college, Duke University, win back-to-back championships in the early 1990s. 1,076 assists.

The kingdom of God is like an assist because those who come out victorious did not do it alone. They have angels to aid them in hurdling obstacles just like the players have teammates who were willing to assist in winning the game. Most champions are

KINGDOM MADNESS

victorious because they involve everyone around them in the process to winning. The teams who make it to "March Madness" play and win as a team. The people who choose to help others make it into the Kingdom of Heaven.

In the kingdom of God, there are many examples of great people who are willing to assist. For example, in the book of Mark (Chapter 2), the word discusses a paralytic man that was sick and crippled. He was carried by four men. They were trying to get him inside of a home where Jesus was. However, these men were not just four men but four friends, four teammates, and four men willing to assist. Their ultimate goal simply was to get to Jesus.

Once they realized they couldn't go through the door of the home, they were willing to assist until their goal was accomplished. Some would view their lack of access into the door as a failed attempt, but these four friends went to the roof of the house and lowered their paralytic friend in for his healing. They exemplified that not only does "teamwork make the dream work", but they exemplified that they must assist through adversity, obstacles, and detours.

In this world, many people had someone who helped them get to their success. The Lone Ranger needed Tonto. The President of the United States needs the Cabinet. Martin Luther King, Jr. needed Ralph Abernathy. When you help others, you help yourself. It is important to note that your end victory cannot be accomplished unless you assist and collaborate with others through the process. Will assists make you famous? Probably not. They will, however, help everyone be successful.

Kingdom Nugget:

"We make a living by what we get, but we make a life by what we give."

~ Winston Churchill

"So they signaled to their partners in the other boat to come and help them. And they came and liked both the boats, so that they begin to sink".

Luke 5:7 NKJV

CHAPTER 5

TEMPO

"In an individual sport, yes, you have to win titles. Baseball's different. But basketball, hockey? One person can control the tempo of a game, can completely alter the momentum of a series. There's a lot of great individual talent."

~Kobe Bryant

Tempo is known to be an important ingredient for good music. Musicians developed a system of useful terms and tempo markings called the metronome: a mechanical device used for keeping time. The tempo can impact the vibe or the spirit of the song.

In basketball, a good coach knows how to not panic if the other team has better players, if everyone is cheering for the opposing team, or if people is booing his team. He understands, that if he can control the tempo, he can increase his chances of winning. Usually, when a team is behind, nothing they planned in practice is working in the game. They are not hitting their shots. They are turning the ball over. What do they do?

A good coach is going to slow the tempo down. This steals the other team's momentum away which allows his team to refocus, get refreshed and execute the game plan without rushing. Players can get comfortable and confident, and the game is now clear. With one play at a time, anything is possible because the tempo is right. At "March Madness", the tempo might be adjusted to pep you or hype you up the expectations of victory. It really does help create a great atmosphere!

The Old Testament reveals stories of pacing and tempo in order to achieve greatness. God took his time, 6 days, to create living creatures and the Earth. It could have been at a faster or slower pace. The meticulous behavior of His actions shows His dedication to something long lasting and precious.

KINGDOM MADNESS

In Joshua 6, trumpets and other blaring noises did not happen until the seventh day. Don't be mistaken: the six days before were not just sitting around and socializing. They marched around with the Ark of the Covenant. Picking the best pace is not just for you; it helps those that you are around know it will happen when it is supposed to happen.

In the New Testament, Hebrews 12: 1-2 reminds us that there will be those who are watching our tempo. We do not need to speed up or slow down because of them, but we do need to remember patience and pace so we can complete the assignment for our life.

I was sitting in the hot Texas heat one day in traffic for 45 minutes. My frustration was high, my patience was low, and I was at a major intersection. As traffic started to move, I noticed the reason for the change of pace: a utility truck was adjusting the traffic light.

I realized something that day: traffic is never a permanent situation. It just needs authority to regulate it and restore order. The traffic light represented the tempo. The light had the ability to slow down or speed up the traffic. The utility truck was the regulator and restorer of order.

In our lives, we get to choose our tempo and GOD helps us to regulate it so we can get back to our regularly scheduled program. So the next time you are delayed at an intersection, remember the tempo change is for your safety and protection. It is also temporary. You will still get to your destination.

Kingdom Nugget: Regardless if you go slow or fast, let GOD help you regulate your pace.

"Therefore, since we are surrounded by such a great cloud of witnesses, let us throw off everything that hinders and the sin that so easily entangles. And let us run with perseverance the race marked out for us, fixing our eyes on Jesus, the pioneer and perfecter of faith. For the joy set before him he endured the cross, scorning its shame, and sat down at the right hand of the throne of God."

Hebrews 12: 1-2 (NIV)

CHAPTER 6

EXECUTION

"Go hard on every play because it could be the play that makes the difference in the game."

~Anonymous

You have "experts" across America that sit in their Lazy Boy recliner and blast coaches every game when a play does not work, and their team falls in defeat. The reality is that the play and the players could have been great, but if the play is not carried out or executed with precision, you won't have the desired results.

Many people desire to get into shape and improve their health and wellness. They purchase the attire. They pay the fee. They talk the talk. The only problem is they don't execute what they have planned due to either distractions or lack of determination. You can have the outer man ready to accomplish the goal, but without an inward transformation, you will not execute them.

In the good book, Jesus was the coach that called many plays. For example, there was a man in the Bible who was blind from birth. After Jesus encountered him and his condition, the play that Jesus called was for the man to go wash his face in the pool of Siloam. Remember, he's blind! The Lazy Boy coaches would probably scream "How is he going to find the pool?" You must learn, like the blind, that there is a kingdom playbook. If it is executed, victory will be manifested. How did the blind man execute it so well if he is blind? Simple. He knew his coach's voice. Even if you are blind, you can win if you respond properly. It will work to your advantage.

I have played sports all my life. The concept of go out and execute is very familiar to my ears. However, you can't just tell me you know the play and expect me to trust that without having seen any evidence of it. Therefore, don't just be gifted in your position, go out and put it into effect. Carry it out according to the play that is being given. In the kingdom of God, I've learned the hard way that many people know the scripture better than the preacher, the bishop, and the apostle. However, they cannot execute scriptures in other people's lives, you're going to have to do that for yourself.

One of the many roadblocks to executing your plans is procrastination, and there are many different types:

- Type 1: The "fun" procrastinator. This person would rather do exciting things and go exciting places rather than buckle down and focus on the task.

- Type 2: The "plenty of time" procrastinator. This person will say "I'll get to it" or "No problem". Then, at the last minute, they rush and, due to frustration, they do a below average job.

- Type 3: The "talkative" procrastinator. This person talks a grand game. They talk about their goals, their plan, and their connections. Their words are fueled by ambition, but their actions are driven by procrastination.

Do not let these procrastination roadblocks keep you keep you from getting whatever your destination will be.

Kingdom Nugget: Don't wait for it...get to it!

"Do not merely listen to the word, and so deceive yourselves. Do what it says."

James 1:22 (NIV)

CHAPTER 7

ALL IN

"Good teams become great ones when the members trust each other enough to surrender the Me for the We."

~ Phil Jackson

Once a team makes it to "March Madness" differences, opinions, and individual thoughts have to be placed on the backburner. It's time to make the dream a reality. The dream is not in need of a star, spectacular plays, or solo players. The dream is in need of a team.

Let's switch to professional basketball for a moment. The 1992 USA Olympic Basketball Team began as a group of amateurs with incredible skills who later became known as "The Dream Team".

Prior to be nationally known they were simply 12 individuals with their own style who came together to represent the United States. What was their key to success? Check the ego. Push for the dream.

In life this is no different from the body of Christ. In "March" or Kingdom Madness, everyone has the same uniform. They have the same game and arena, but they may not have the same agenda. It's like when people say "Teamwork makes the dream work", but the dream doesn't work because the whole team does not have the same dream. You should not strive just look like a team, but you should operate as a team. A team has victory in sight, and the players are locked into a united accomplishment. It is not about me, myself, and I but it's about the team as whole and the role each individual plays that involved

Jesus could not be a coach without a team. So, He went in search of disciples: people who spread the Word for others to hear and accept. At the beginning of His search, there were 72 disciples sent out to deliver the Word (Luke 10: 1-23). They were given the tools and script to explain to those who would hear it. By the time we get to the last supper, however, highlighted were only the 12. We do know that those 12 disciples ended up becoming some of Jesus' greatest

KINGDOM MADNESS

confidants because of their dedication to the end goal which was salvation. Were these 12 disciples perfect? Absolutely not. They had to learn the power of teamwork. But their willingness to try was all Jesus needed.

As you attempt to accomplish your goals, you are going to have someone or a group that will be a part of your success. You are not going to do it all by yourself. You want to surround yourself with people that understand that success for you is a success for everyone.

So how do you know who is willing to work with the team and who is not? Consider these steps as you create your "dream team":

1. Find people who celebrate you and not just tolerate you. They are excited to see you excel and they are willing to help when you fail.

2. Find people who are smarter or wiser than you. These people will help challenge you so you can be better and do better. You cannot grow if you cannot learn.

3. Find people who will not weigh you or your team down with unproductivity. If they do not contribute or are there just

for the times they can benefit, let them go.

Think of it like an airplane. An airplane can only have a certain amount of weight before it will not be able to fly properly. If these people are causing you to not reach your altitude, lighten your flight.

Creating a team where everyone is "all in" is going to be difficult because appearance can be deceiving. However, you must be diligent in getting rid of people who are dead weight, unbalanced, and not stepping in the same timing as you. It's like the author Arketa Williams once said, "Just because a person smiles in your face, hugs you, and says "I love you" doesn't mean they have your best interest at heart." Teamwork is humility over pride. It is sharing over selfishness. It is having an "all in" mentality.

Kingdom Nugget:

"Make sure everyone in your boat is rowing and not drilling holes when you're not looking."

~ Steve Maraboli

Two are better than one, because they have a good return for their labor: If either of them falls down, one can help the other up. But pity anyone who falls and has no one to help them up.

>Ecclesiastes 4:9-10 (NIV)

CHAPTER 8

THE MINDSET OF THE UNDERDOG

"I like being the underdog, so they don't expect what's going to happen. It pushes me to work harder and do the things I'm not doing better."

~Kawhi Leonard

April 1, 1985 Villanova University's Wildcat Basketball team beats Georgetown University 66 to 64 to clench the NCAA Basketball Championship.

What makes Villanova so special?

    a. They had an "okay" season record: 19-10.

    b. They barely qualified for the "March Madness" tournament.

c. Each game leading up to the championship was won by less than 5 points.

This school was not a basketball power house. April 1, 1985, however, changed the game forever. They were officially a prime example of how underdogs can win.

The term "underdog" is defined as "A competitor thought to have little to no chance of winning". Typically, they are not popular. They are inadequate. Most people do not pay attention to them because they are not considered a threat.

Does that sound familiar? If it does, please know you are not alone. A lot of people are counted out just by appearance or lifestyle.

If I could, I would rename Hebrews 11 "The Underdog Chapter". The whole chapter discusses many underdogs of the Bible and the one attribute they had in common: Faith. They believed, even though it could have killed them, made them poor, or emotionally damage them.

One of those underdogs was Abraham. At 100 years of age, God said that Abraham would have a baby with Sarah. Did they question this possibility? Absolutely. There were no drugs like Viagra or Cialis. Sarah couldn't go to a clinic and go through an invitro process. Their faith, however, was stronger than their doubt. As a result of their faith, Abraham became the father to many nations.

Hebrews 11:1 encourages us to have faith even when you cannot see it or know it. Abraham's hope activated his faith which led to his success. There may be people who do not understand. You may even have concerns. Let your hope be the force that drives your faith in order to get to your victory.

There have (or will be) people in your life who will attempt to belittle you or make you feel inadequate. They will decide that because you don't have the appearance, intelligence, common sense, skill, or proper background that you are not qualified to succeed. They have counted you out, but God is ready to lead you to the win.

The Mindset of the Underdog takes 3 simple steps:

1. Remember that God is a part of your team. If HE is with you, what can be against you?

2. Say yes to Him even when it makes no sense to you. If He can deliver Gideon, He can do the same for you.

3. Know that you are the overcomer. Yes, man might see you as the underdog, but God sees you as Victorious!

Kingdom Nugget: Underdogs are God's favorite winners.

"Finally, brothers and sisters, whatever is true, whatever is noble, whatever is right, whatever is pure, whatever is lovely, whatever is admirable — if anything is excellent or praiseworthy — think about such things."

Philippians 4:8 (NIV)

CHAPTER 9

WINNERS MAKE ADJUSTMENTS

"If you are not doing it the right way, why are you doing it? Learn how to do it the right way and practice it the right way."

~Anonymous

Halftime. It isn't just for commercials, commentary from old basketball players, and cheer squad routines. It gives teams a chance to relax and possibly reset.

In "March Madness," I have observed several teams complete halftime adjustments. The team comes into the game full of confidence and ready to play, but the first half of the game does not work in their favor. They play the wrong defense. Their shots are not going into the basket. They continuously foul.

These teams use halftime to acknowledge their mistakes, change their playing style, and do better in the second half. Many of the greatest coaches have elevated their value and respect from their players because of their halftime adjustment.

A prime example of adjusting in times of trouble is the tale of Gideon and his 300 men (Judges 7). Gideon was a no name guy. He was young. He collected grains and made wines for a living. God sent an angel to tell him to lead an army against the Midianites.

Please understand that Gideon had NO clue about armies and wars, but he also knew that God would never put him in a place to forsake him. So, Gideon accepted the call and trusted God.

He started with 32,000 men in his army. God told him, "Too many. Downsize." Gideon did as God asked, and his army went from 32,000 to 10,000. God looked and said, "Eh...still too many. Downsize."

I'm sure Gideon had a really confused look on his face, but he did as God asked. His army decreased from 10,000 to 300. God finally said "Perfect! Let's go to war." Gideon went to war with his 300 men...and WON. Gideon's victory proves that adjustment can be adding, subtracting, changing, reinventing, etc. In other words, there are different ways to adjust. YOU have to decide to listen to the voice of God and do what works best for you. In doing so, you must also understand that the method you chose won't necessarily look like what someone else have done either but will be unique to your own experience.

I was in Atlanta, Georgia for a business trip. My attire was casual since I was visiting some of my favorite places that did not include a dress code. The evening of my last night, however, did call for a professional dress code since I was delivering a speech. I had one problem: I had NO suit.

I went out to purchase a suit, but it needed alterations. I researched and found a location that would be able to alter my suit. When I arrived at the tailor, I immediately got discouraged because there were several people in front of me.

I didn't want to be late to my engagement, but I also did not want to look unkept. As I was impatiently waiting, the owner asked me why I was in town. I told him I was from Dallas and I was in Atlanta to speak to some young men about raising their expectations to success.

KINGDOM MADNESS

It was then that the owner gave me words to live by. He said, "Be patient. Stay calm. Focus on your assignment. True winners make adjustments in order to complete their task."

I meditated on his words. He was right. I sat down and prepared myself for my speech. By the time I finished preparing, I had my suit, a new business friend, and my motivational speech for my engagement.

In Kingdom Madness, you can have your life planned to go one way. You knew that by the time you reached a certain age that you were going to accomplish all your goals. You knew that your first marriage will be your only marriage. You knew that you would be at a certain job for life.

Then, you get to 35 and realize you haven't accomplished 1/3 of your list. Your marriage is on its last leg, and your company had to downsize so you were laid off. Things did not go the exact way you expected them to, but it did not deter you from making the best out of what you have experienced.

First, you practiced humility to combat the pride that wants you to stay stuck in mediocrity. Then, you adjusted your goals. You worked with your partner to rebuild a healthy relationship. You found a better job with better pay and benefits. You made your halftime adjustments throughout life in order to get to the victory you deserve.

Kingdom Nugget: Adjustments might not be pleasurable, but adjustments have purpose.

"Therefore, we do not lose heart. Though outwardly we are wasting away, yet inwardly we are being renewed day by day. 17 For our light and momentary troubles are achieving for us an eternal glory that far outweighs them all."

2 Corinthians 4: 16-17

CHAPTER 10

FATIGUED BUT FOCUSED

"It's the little details that are vital, little things make big things happen."

~ John Wooten

Breathe. You are almost at the finish line. It is the last 30 seconds of the game. The game is tied and there is one second left. You are on the free throw line to shoot two shots. You make one, and the victory is yours.

The problem: you're drained, tired, and fatigued. The crowd is loud. There is booing and cheering. The lights are bright. All eyes are on you. Your heart is beating fast. Your hands are sweaty, and your coach calls a time out to gather the team for this big moment that will go down in history.

There are a couple of things to notice about the coach in this time out:

1. The coach represents the voice of authority. He gets the team to relax. In life when things like family crisis or job stress arise, the voice of authority, God, is saying to relax in order to bring peace to your weary mind.

2. The coach reminds the one shooting to remember to bend his knees before the shot. In the kingdom, we must remember to seek peace and bend our knees in prayer. This is how our second burst of strength comes from.

3. The final thing that the coach will say is simply "Breathe". Remembering to breathe and gain your second wind because your victory relies on it. Stop to take a deep breath and exhale. Your focus will improve which means your percentages of winning increase.

While it appears that the timeout is for the coach, it is for the players to get focused for the win. There was a lady in the Good Book (Luke 8: 43-48) that had an issue she was dealing with for twelve years. It was an issue no doctor, no specialist, or no herbal supplement could help. She exemplified how you accomplish your miracle.

She first had to be alert and aware when the opportunity for a miracle was near. She knew a man name Jesus was coming by. Do you let opportunities pass you by because you're not alert or aware?

She secondly forgot about the twelve years of failed attempts for her miracle of healing and said, "This is my day for a miracle." In life, you must understand that if God allowed you to witness a new day that there's a chance for a miracle in your life.

It starts in the mind. Speak positively. Put positive words in the atmosphere. This lady said, "If I could just touch the hem of his garment, I know I'll be made whole."

Thirdly, she pushed past the crowd determined that this was her one shot at a miracle. Her one shot to transform from issues controlling her to miracles uplifting her. This could be your day for your miracle!

George Bernard Shaw said it best, "A miracle is an event which creates faith. That is the purpose and nature of miracles. Frauds deceive. An event which creates faith does not deceive therefore, it is not a fraud, but a miracle."

In "March Madness", I have observed it's exciting to the fans game after game. The ratings are through the roof for the networks, but these teams and players must stay focused through the cheers, the boos, the injuries, and the delays in the start times. Truth is anyone can stay focused when you're fresh, focused, and rested, but can you stay focused when tired, drained, and fatigued?

What makes others filled with joy can cause others fatigue. "March Madness" is at a point of the season where players are really drained mentally and beat up physically. What's taking place is that they are reaping the benefits of sowing or giving all, they could in the offseason, training, the preseason, and the ups and down of the regular season.

They approached it like the Kingdom Book instructed in Luke 14:28, "Suppose one of you wants to build a tower. Won't you first sit down and estimate the cost to see if you have enough money to complete it?"

In other words, you have to prepare and focus before you can execute anything. Focus needs a few things to keep from being disrupted.

1. Keep the big picture. If you are at the movies, you can get caught into the popcorn, candy, drinks, previews, and more previews. You forget that you are there for the main event, the big picture. Too many previews can exhaust you before the main attraction. Stay focused.

2. Keep your mind from wandering and drifting from the goal. Guard what goes into your ears. What you hear can impact can cause a lack of focus. Don't seek to hear too much hype about yourself or too much criticism about yourself.

3. Tunnel vision can be viewed as negative because you can only do one thing at a time. But to accomplish the big picture, you need tunnel vision: the ability to block out distractions in front and side of you.

Kingdom Nugget: Press beyond the crowd for your kingdom miracle.

"He gives strength to the weary and increases the power of the weak."

Isaiah 40:29

CHAPTER 11
EXPECT THE UNEXPECTED

"Like life, basketball is messy and unpredictable. It has its way with you, no matter how hard you try to control it. The trick is to experience each moment with a clear mind and an open heart. When you do that, the game–and life–will take care of itself"

~Phil Jackson

You can practice 1000 free throws. You can run zone defense strategies millions of times. No matter how much you repeat drills and skills, it does not guarantee victory. Basketball games are unpredictable, but those skills and drills help you to manage what may happen more efficiently.

The worst thing, however, to hear after a defeat is "Well...we thought we were prepared, but this play or player caught us off-guard." How can you be caught off-guard? You didn't expect the unexpected. Sometimes, you can be so focus on so many things in the game (and in life) that you overlook simple things.

The Bible is full of unexpected blessings that usually came to those who trusted Him even though they could not trace him.

Jesus called the disciples to follow Him. They did not know where. They did not know the good or bad consequences. They trusted Him, and that was all that most of them needed.

As they experienced the journey with Him, they learned that their choice to follow Him came with some unexpected twists and turns. Nonetheless, they stayed focused and continued their journey. When opposition did cross their path, they did not panic. The disciples remembered the unexpected miracles of Jesus like turning water into wine (John 2:1-11) or feeding 5,000 hungry people (Matthew 14:13-21). Those miracles taught them that God will do the unexpected and to be prepared for the works that will ultimately have a positive outcome. So don't lose faith or become weary in what you're doing. Rest assured that God has a plan for everything we go through to work together for our good. Just keep the faith!

Life is a daily experience of unexpected happenings. Will you get to the graduation stage? Will you get that promotion? Will you have that baby? Will you get paid for your services? How do you prepare for what is to come?

Think about how thousands of teams prepare to play a game of basketball. You practice drills and skills to help you adjust better on the fly to what will come your way.

Here are three skills you can practice for the unexpected:

1. Preparation. How many times have you booked a trip way in advanced like one year or so? As it creeps closer to the actual departure, you slowly get excited and you have great expectations. Since you booked it so far ahead, you do not really concern yourself with packing or discussing what you intend to do on the trip.

Then, when the day of the trip arrives, you are rushing and stressed because you did not prepare for traffic, detours, or even gate changes. Preparation is continuous from initial start to the finish. If you prepare for the unexpected, it will display itself in your preparation.

KINGDOM MADNESS

2. Perception. Popeye The Sailor. He is hands down one of the greatest cartoon characters ever! His constant struggle was protecting his pride and joy, Olive Oyl, from the mighty clutches of Brutus, the strong and obviously more athletic character in the cartoon.

Brutus always believed that his brawns could get him anything and anyone he wanted including Olive Oyl. Because of this belief, he always underestimated Popeye's abilities. Popeye was short and scrawny, so Brutus perceived him to be non-threatening. A lot of times, you act like Brutus. You think that because it has never happened to you or things are going so well for you that you are ok.

Perceptions like this are exactly how life can catch you off-guard. Then, you experience the defeat Brutus experiences every time he went against Popeye after Popeye ate his spinach. Do not allow your perception of your opponent (life, a person, or a condition) keep you from being able to adjust.

3. Progress. Successful building companies know that it is not who builds the biggest or most flamboyant buildings

that is able to endure economic ups and downs. It is the builder who is consistent. Their projects have a consistent flow. They prepare for unexpected weather issues or circumstance. The preparation for the unexpected leads to progress. Progress can only happen if you continue to move forward even after the unexpected happens.

The victory in your life can only come when you prepare, perceive, and progress to success. It is NOT going to be easy. Kingdom Madness requires you to struggle in order to get better. Don't be overconfident. Practice your drills and skills so whatever may happen you are ready to battle.

Kingdom Nugget: Never underestimate your challenge. Take it seriously.

"But stay awake at all times, praying that you may have strength to escape all these things that are going to take place, and to stand before the Son of Man."

Luke 21:36 (ESV)

CHAPTER 12

TURNOVERS

"Chance favors those in motion."

~James H. Austin

You are glued to the television screen watching two amazing college teams go tit-for-tat in a semi-final game. The ball is moving like a comet around the court. Players are pushing and setting up screens so their players can get closer to the rim and... **WHISTLE BLOWN.**

A high pitch screech fills the gym. The referee points to a player near the goal and holds out three fingers. It was a Three Second Violation.

Then, the referee points to the other side of the court. The other team throws the ball into play and starts running down the court.

The team on defense is ready and meets the ball handler at half court. His defense is aggressive and full of movement. It is so aggressive that the ball handler must step back to see who he can throw the ball to and WHISTLE BLOWN.

You look for the referee and you see him making this rolling motion with his arms. This team went backcourt. Then, the referee points to the other side of the court. You sit frustrated. How can both teams make such simple mistakes like that? In the game of basketball, turnovers happen.

Three second violations in basketball happen when the team on offense has a player that spends too much time by the goal instead of moving around to attempt to score a basket. I watched a game one year during "March Madness" when the team that won should not have won.

The team that lost had superior talent, a better record, and the odds were in their favor to win. Why did they lose? They had more violation than the other team. What were most of the violations? Three second violations! Someone on their team could not keep the flow of the play in order to score points.

Backcourt violations happen when a team member that is already on their side of the court moving toward the goal somehow goes back to their opponent's side of the court. I have played basketball my entire life, and I was always reminded of one important rule: Never go back. Do not go backcourt. Do not lose your focus because of where you have been.

Both violations are due to confusion and uncertainty. Somewhere in the game, the players lose focus of the goal: winning. This happened A LOT when Jesus was on Earth because people were uncertain of who He was or what He could do. During the time Jesus was on His way to crucifixion, a lot of people were unsure of who He was. (John 7:25-44) Many people, those who knew Him and did not, questioned whether He was the son of God.

Jesus, however, knew His followers apart from others. In John 7:38, He explains that those who believe in Him "...rivers of living water will flow from within them." In other words, those who know who He is will continuously represent His truth and His beliefs. They do not wait to spread the word or to have faith. It is already a part of who they are.

Life has many instances where we get stuck in neutral, and we are just spinning our wheels. We lose sight of where we are and where we should be. It leaves us stagnant. It is almost like parking in a place we know we should not be parking. If we stay there too long, we may have to financially pay for it. There is nothing wrong with staying still for a certain period, but after a while, we need to keep it moving.

Three seconds in the paint and backcourt violations are really a case of hesitation. It can be the demise of your destiny or your goal. Hesitation feels good at first, but it can cost you the ultimate victory that He wants for you.

In the words of the late, great, Kobe Bryant, *you must be quick and swift in making your cuts to move towards the goal. Always be in motion toward your future, desires, or goals. Keep your vision and dreams.* When you lose sight of where you are going, refocus and remember that slow motion is better than no motion. Get out the paint, get out of neutral and get going!

Kingdom Nugget: Move like a river and not like a pond.

"Have I not commanded you? Be strong and courageous. Do not be frightened, and do not be dismayed, for the Lord your God is with you wherever you go."

Joshua 1:9 (ESV)

Jesus replied, "No one who puts a hand to the plow and looks back is fit for service in the kingdom of God."

Luke 9:62

CHAPTER 13

BEWARE OF THE CHEERS

"The time when there is no one there to feel sorry for you or to cheer for you is when a player is made."

~Tim Duncan

In "March Madness", fans are everything. They go berserk. It is complete madness in the form of uncontrollable joy and excitement.

Have you ever considered that all cheers are not for the players? Some cheers are for the school or for the coach. As a player, you must have the ability to encourage yourself because not everyone is around to cheer for your success.

The Good Book displays how to not get caught up in cheers. In Mark 11:9-11, Jesus entered Jerusalem on Palm Sunday to the

KINGDOM MADNESS

cheers and salutations. While the cheering was great and appreciated, Jesus had to stay focused on his mission. He knew that the same people wishing him success would be the same people wishing for His death.

Cheers are a result of an internal emotional response that is expressed externally. During the Kingdom Madness, you must create your inner joy and operate in the role that has been designed for you. This joy allows you to keep progressing through chaos, crisis, and challenges along the way.

The absolute one thing you can NOT depend on are what I call your "emotional gears". In a car, you can shift your car into several gears: Drive, Reverse, or Neutral. When people cheer your success, they appreciate your DRIVE, but they may not be around for your failures.

You also have people who like to boo and speak negativity against you. Those people intend to REVERSE you back to who you used to be. And even when you are in NEUTRAL waiting to make your next move, people may try to make you move faster or slower than what is needed. You must eliminate the emotional fears in your life and go forward knowing the God has a role for you.

There are also cheers that intend to distract your focus from your goals. It's kind of like when people make noise while a person is attempting a free throw. When this happens, you must boost your drive and use your determination. Determination helps you to tune out the cheers and jeers so you can work within your joy. Your joy will give you strength.

Kingdom Nugget: It's does not matter if they are cheering or booing, find the strength to Do YOU.

"I can do All things through Christ who strengthens me."

Philippians 4:13

CHAPTER 14

ONE SHOT

"I've missed more than 9000 shots in my career. I've lost almost 300 games. 26 times, I've been trusted to take the game winning shot and missed. I've failed over and over and over again in my life. And that is why I succeed."

~Michael Jordan

Duke University's Christian Laetner. Villanova University's Kris Jenkins. North Carolina State University's Lorenzo Charles. These three gentlemen recognized during "March Madness" that if there is time on the clock there is still a chance for one shot.

Their last shots were also the shots that gave their teams the victory in their games. A team can be behind the entire game, but one shot can change the outcome. It is not a matter of how you started the game. The ending is the most important.

In the Bible, there are many examples of "one shot blessings". These are events that at the last second changed a bible character's life. Take David for example. (1 Samuel 17) He was a little shepherd boy. Nobody had any expectations for him to succeed.

In fact, people expected him to be destroyed by the giant Goliath. David knew the odds were stacked against him. He knew he wasn't favored by people, but GOD favored him. David approached his opposition with 5 smooth stones. In one shot, David had conquered the giant. That one shot changed David's life.

There are many who have degrees and hours of education along with support from family, but their lives are not going the way they expected. Then, you have those no family, no degree, and no high school diploma with thriving businesses and success. How does this happen?

They did not focus on what society owed them. They did not feel entitled to anything. They took a shot and went for what they wanted.

Just like unexpected teams end up in the "March Madness" tournament, you can experience the same unexpected results. Those unexpected teams play with a sense of enthusiasm that indicates their appreciation for the one shot they have at victory.

God reminds us that we are not entitled to greatness. His grace and his mercy allows us one shot at all the blessings and promises in the kingdom.

Kingdom Nugget: Don't give up. Don't throw in the towel. There is still time on the clock for one shot.

"Let us not become weary in doing good, for at the proper time we will reap a harvest if we do not give up."

Galatians 6:9

CHAPTER 15

CROWNING MOMENT

"To win, you've got to put the ball in the macramé."

~Terry McGuire

Ah...the victory. After all the stress, excitement, challenges, ups, downs, injuries, and agony; ONE team is left standing. Most teams, after winning the NCAA Basketball Tournament ("March Madness") complete a tradition called "cutting the net".

Each member of the team cuts a piece of the net from the goal post. The coach usually cuts the last piece of the net, and the team keeps this as a memento of their adventure to victory. If you think about it, it is kind of weird.

The very thing that determined whether you scored and advanced is the one thing you want to keep. Why? Why would someone want to remember all that pain and anguish? Because it is in YOUR control when you win. What you were once a slave to is now in your hands to remind you that struggle can lead to victory.

Chapter 14 of this book explained how David, a little shepherd boy, used his one shot to kill the giant Goliath. (1 Samuel 17) After he killed the giant, David ran, stood over the giant, took a huge sword, and cut the giant's head off. David wanted a reminder of what used to control him and his people.

It was a symbol of their past: their past poverty, their past intimidation, and their past fears. Could you imagine David walking through the city with this in his hand?! That was a crowning moment.

It does not matter how long you have been going through tribulations in your life. If you can believe in God, you can be certain that your crowning moment can start today! Victory is not just materialistic things like a house, cars, clothes, and excessive amounts of friends.

Victory is the day you get up from whatever had you down, and you choose to go forward from one word of God. What will be your crowning moment? What will be your memento of struggle to success? What will be your victory?

Kingdom Nugget: The glory of the victorious CROWN, starts with the challenges of the daily CROSS.

"No, in all these things we are more than conquerors through him who loved us."

Romans 8:37 (ESV)

SPECIAL THANKS

I want to thank my one and only son Tony for his writing contribution and ideas to the book.

Thank you to my daughter Jasmine, my baby girl, for organizing, formatting, and editing my writing. You always helped process my thoughts.

I'd like to thank my writing guide Arketa Williams for the knowledge and inspiration that helped me elevate to another level in my writing as an author.

Thank you Pastor King for being a mentor that always showed me love and compassion.

Thank you Pastor Dwight McKissick for opening the doors of many opportunities within the kingdom. I was able to learn, advance, and encounter a higher level of ministry through your leadership.

Thank you Pastor Conway Edwards for

your transparent teachings and leadership skills that has helped me develop as a man of God, Pastor, and leader.

Thank you Gerald Alley, CEO of Con-Real, LP for the words of inspiration in being a leader and developing leaders.

Last but not least, special thank you to my beautiful wife Angela of 30 years for assisting me through the process every step of the way. She is my manager and has managed the process. I wouldn't be where I am without her.

A special thanks to my parents, James and Evelyn Tucker; my in-laws, Calvin and Geraldine Joubert; my two grandsons, Aston and Ryley; and to my church family, The Inspired Church.

GET CONNECTED WITH AUTHOR ANTHONY TUCKER SR. ON SOCIAL MEDIA.

 Instagram.com/atuckersr

 Facebook/AuthorAnthonyTucker

REFERENCE

"Bobby Hurley College Stats: College Basketball at Sports." *Reference.com,* 2000, www.reference.com/cbb/players/bobby-hurley-1.html.

KINGDOM MADNESS

www.ingramcontent.com/pod-product-compliance
Lightning Source LLC
Chambersburg PA
CBHW071914070526
44583CB00016B/1989